The questions from
has been taken from
year and created for
responsible for the accuracy of the information in the
questions and answers.

There are various ways to play this game with a group of
people.

## Party Version

- If you have a group of people over you can simply
  read out the question, then the 4 choices as an
  entertaining pastime with no winners and losers.
  This would require 1 person to be the reader of the
  question only to see if anyone can guess the correct
  answer. If nobody guesses correctly, the reader
  would then read the 4 choices before providing the
  answers.

## Trivia Night

- For Trivia Night, you can randomly pick 20 questions
  where the reader, reads the questions out with the 4
  choices. The participants write their answers from 1
  to 20 and then at the end of the 20 questions, you can
  review all of the answers to see who the winner is.
  You can rotate the reader so everyone has a chance to
  play.

## Travel Trivia

- Similar to the Party Version but played in the car on
  long road trips to pass the time. Someone other than
  the driver is the reader.

# TOP 100 HITS 70's & 80's QUESTIONS

1/ Finish the lyrics from the 1985 Mr. Mister song "Broken Wings" -
"Take these broken wings and learn to fly again,____ ____ ____ ____
____ "

- "learn to love again"
- "want you hear with me"
- "learn to live so free"
- "fly high above the tree"

2/ What 1966 Supremes hit did Phil Collins cover in 1982?

- "You Can't Hurry Love"
- "Where Did Our Love Go"
- "A Groovy Kind Of Love"
- "Baby Love"

3/ Who released the song "He ain't Heavy, He's My Brother" in 1969?

- The Hollies
- Wet Wet Wet
- Cliff Richard
- Glenn Medeiros

4/ Name the Song with the lyrics "The first time ever I saw your face. I
thought the sun rose in your eyes, and the moon and stars were the gifts
you gave" (1972)

- "The First Time Ever I Saw Your Face"
- "Your Face"
- "The First Time"
- "Annie's Song"

**5/ Who had a #1 hit and #26 bestselling song of 1989 titled "Blame It On The Rain"?**

- Bobby Brown
- Milli Vanilli
- Fine Young Cannibals
- Michael Damien

**6/ In 1983 what band released "Talking In Your Sleep"?**

- Duran Duran
- Prince and The Revolution
- The Romantics
- Thompson Twins

**7/ What artist released "Never Gonna Give You Up" in 1987 becoming the #4 bestselling song of the year in the U.S.?**

- Rick Astley
- Spandau Ballett
- George Michael
- Robert Palmer

**8/ Who covered the 1988 song "Girl You Know It's True"?**

- Bobby Brown
- Richard Marx
- Milli Vanilli
- Prince

**9/ Who released the 1972 song "Schools Out"?**

- Slade
- T. Rex
- Gary Glitter
- Alice Cooper

**10/ What group released "Eternal Flame" in 1989?**

- The Hollies
- The Bangles
- The Go-Go's
- Queen

**11/ What band released "Don't You (Forget About Me)" in 1982?**

- Simple Minds
- Tears For Fears
- Pet Shop Boys
- Duran Duran

**12/ What group released the song "Give A Little Bit" in 1977?**

- Bay City Rollers
- Spinners
- Supertramp
- Steve Miller Band

**13/ Finish the lyrics to the 1986 song "Lady in red, is dancing with me _____ _____ _____"**

- just you and me
- cheek to cheek
- holding me tight
- feeling the beat

**14/ Who released the song "Rocket Man" in 1972?**

- David Bowie
- Elton John
- Ziggy Pop
- The Who

**15/ What male singer released the song "Superstition" in 1973?**

- Stevie Wonder
- Paul Simon
- Al Wilson
- Billy Preston

**16/ Who had the #40 song of 1970 titled "Love Grows (Where my Rosemary Goes)"?**

- Tony Orlando and Dawn
- Edison Lighthouse
- Dion
- The Archies

**17/ In 1976, who released the song "Saturday Night"?**

- Bay City Rollers
- Whigfield
- The Proclaimers
- Simple Minds

**18/ Name the song with the lyrics - "Watching every motion in my foolish lover's game. On this endless ocean finally lovers know no shame" (1986)**

- "Endless Love"
- "Top Gun"
- "Caravan Of Love"
- "Take My Breath Away"

**19/ What band released the song "Layla" in 1971?**

- Derek and the Dominos
- Eric Clapton
- Jackson Browne
- Steely Dan

**20/ Who had the hit song "Only In My Dreams" in 1987?**

- Tiffany
- Debbie Gibson
- Belinda Carlisle
- Debbie Boone

**21/ Who released the song "Our Lips Are Sealed" in 1981?**

- The Bangles
- Fun Boy Three
- The Go-Go's
- Hilary and Haylie Duff

**22/ The song "Hello" was released in 1984 by who?**

- George Michael
- Stevie Wonder
- Eurythmics
- Lionel Richie

**23/ Name the group who had the 1987 hit song title "Notorious"?**

- Cutting Crew
- Prince
- Duran Duran
- Huey Lewis and the News

**24/ "December 1963 (Oh, What a Night)" was released in 1975 by what group?**

- The Four Seasons
- The Beach Boys
- Showaddywaddy
- Brotherhood of Man

**25/ Who sung the #2 song for 1974 titled "Seasons In The Sun"?**

- Susan Jacks
- The Poppy Family
- Paper Lace
- Terry Jacks

**26/ Name the song with the lyrics - "Last night I dreamt of San Pedro, just like I'd never gone, I new the song" (1987)**

- "Papa Don't Preach"
- "La Isla Bonita"
- "True Blue"
- "Open Your Heart"

**27/ What singer/group released the #12 song for 1989 titled "Waiting For A Star To Fall"?**

- Richard Marx
- Milli Vanilli
- Bad English
- Boy Meets Girl

**28/ What is it that is multiplyin' in the 1978 song "You're The One That I Want"?**

- Thrills
- Chills
- Bills
- Pills

**29/ Who released "One Night In Bangkok" in 1984?**

- Animotion
- John Parr
- Murray Head
- Scandal

**30/ In 1986, Gregory Abbott released what #1 hit song? (It reached #3 for Bestselling songs of 1987)**

- "I Got The Feelin' (It's Over)"
- "Shake You Down"
- "Alone"
- "Let Me Be Your Hero"

**31/ What band released "Owner of a Lonely Heart" in 1983?**

- Genesis
- Van Halen
- Yes
- 10 CC

**32/ Who released the song "Clap For The Wolfman" in 1974?**

- Bachman Turner Overdrive
- Burton Cummings
- The Guess Who
- Randy Bachman

**33/ What band released "Never Can Say Goodbye" in 1971?**

- The Osmonds
- Stevie Wonder
- Fifth Dimension
- Jackson Five

**34/ Who had the Number 1 song for 1978 called "Shadow Dancing"?**

- The Bee Gees
- Andy Gibb
- Exile
- Eric Clapton

## 35/ What band released the song "Signs" in 1971?

- Chicago
- Dr. Hook
- Nitty Gritty Dirt Band
- Five Man Electrical Band

## 36/ Who released the song "When Doves Cry" in 1984?

- Lionel Richie
- Kenny Loggins
- Culture Club
- Prince

## 37/ Name the song with the lyrics - "Hey, once I was a funky singer, playin' in a Rock and Roll Band. I never had no problem" (1976)

- "Play That Funky Music"
- "Love Machine"
- "Superstition"
- "December 1963"

## 38/ Who released "Another Brick In The Wall" in 1979?

- Led Zepplin
- Police
- David Bowie
- Pink Floyd

## 39/ In 1971 who released the song "Brand New Key"?

- Melanie
- Judy Collins
- Freda Payne
- Helen Reddy

**40/ What Duet released the song "Leather And Lace" in 1981?**

- Waylon Jennings and Jessi Colter
- Kenny Rogers and Sheena Easton
- Terry Jacks and Susan Jacks
- Stevie Nicks and Don Henley

**41/ What female singer released "Self Control" in 1984?**

- Debbie Gibson
- Laura Branigan
- Sheila E
- Madonna

**42/ Which Band covered Roy Orbison's song "Oh Pretty Woman" in 1982?**

- Little River Band
- Loverboy
- Prince
- Van Halen

**43/ Name the song with the lyrics - "All the old pain'tings on the tombs, they do the sand dance don't you know" (1986)**

- "Paradise"
- "Arabian Knights"
- "Walk Like An Egyptian"
- "Eternal Flame"

**44/ Name the singer/group who released the song "I'll Be There For You" in 1989?**

- Aerosmith
- Bryan Adams
- Simply Red
- Bon Jovi

**45/ In 1985, who released the song "Part-Time Lover"?**

- Lionel Richie
- Billy Ocean
- Phil Collins
- Stevie Wonder

**46/ Name the group who released the song "Hungry Like The Wolf" in 1983?**

- Simple Minds
- Duran Duran
- Journey
- Naked Eyes

**47/ What group released the song "I Still Haven't Found What I'm looking For" in 1987?**

- Duran Duran
- Simple Minds
- Genesis
- U2

**48/ What group released "Funkytown" in 1980?**

- Lipps Inc.
- Pseudo Echo
- Tierra
- Chicago

**49/ Name the song with the lyrics - "I can think of younger days, when living for my life was everything a man could want to do" ( 1971)**

- "Lonely Days"
- "Melody Fair"
- "How Can You Mend A Broken Heart"
- "Run To Me"

**50/ How many times did Tony Orlando want to knock on the pipe in his 1971 song "Knock Three Times"?**

- Twice
- Four Times
- Once
- Three Times

**51/ Name The Song with the lyrics - "I Have a picture pinned to my wall. An image of you and me and we're laughing and loving it all" ( 1983)**

- "Doctor Doctor"
- "King For A Day"
- "Hold Me Now"
- "Lay Your Hands On Me"

**52/ What 1962 Roy Orbison song did Don McLean cover in 1980?**

- "Crying"
- "Pretty Woman"
- "Only The Lonely
- "It's Over"

**53/ "Spirit In The Sky" was released by who in 1969?**

- Doctor and the Medics
- Lee Marvin
- Norman Greenbaum
- T. Rex

**54/ Name The Song with the lyrics - "What I want, you've got, and it might be hard to handle. But like the flame that burns the candle. The candle feeds the flame" (1981)**

- "You Make My Dreams"
- "Maneater"
- "Out Of Touch"
- "Private Eyes"

**55/ "Holding Back the Years" was released in 1982 by "The Frantic Elevators" The band re-released the song in 1985 under what name?**

- Simply Red
- Starship
- Human League
- Pet Shop Boys

**56/ In 1979 what male singer released the song "Cars"?**

- Rod Stewart
- Gary Numan
- Cliff Richard
- David Bowie

**57/ Who covered the song "Saving All My Love For You" in 1985?**

- Whitney Houston
- Marilyn McCoo & Billy Davis Jr.
- Phyllis Nelson
- Elain Paige

**58/ Name the song with the lyrics - "Kissing like a bandit, Stealing time, Underneath a sycamore tree" (1988)**

- "Wishing Well"
- "One More Try"
- "Get Outta My Dreams, Get Into My Car"
- "Simply Irresistible"

**59/ Who covered the song "Always On My Mind" in 1987?**

- Willie Nelson
- Pet Shop Boys
- Ray Charles
- George Michaels

**60/ Name the song with the lyrics - "Sleight of hand and twist of fate, on a bed of nails she makes me wait" (1987)**

- "Livin' on a Prayer"
- "With Or Without You"
- "Don't Dream Till It's Over"
- "I Still Haven't Found What I'm Looking For"

**61/ What male artist released the song "Little Red Corvette" in 1983?**

- Lionel Richie
- Billy Joel
- Phil Collins
- Prince

**62/ Who released the song titled "Space Oddity" in 1972?**

- Queen
- Ziggy Stardust
- Bryan Ferry
- David Bowie

**63/ Name The Song with the lyrics - "A long, long time ago, I can still remember how that music used to make me smile" (Released in 1971 & covered in 1999)**

- "American Pie"
- "The Day The Music Died"
- "A Long, Long Time Ago"
- "Bye Bye"

**64/ What band released the song "I Want To Know What Love Is" in 1984?**

- Hall and Oates
- Foreigner
- Aerosmith
- Van Halen

**65/ In the 1989 song "Stand" by R.E.M., In the first line, where do they tell you to stand?**

- Stand in the place where you work
- Stand in the place where you live
- Stand with your feet on the ground
- Stand in the place where you were

**66/ The song "(They Long To Be) Close To You" was the #2 song for 1970 was sung by who?**

- Captain and Tennille
- Lynn Anderson
- The Carpenters
- Freda Payne

**67/ Who wrote and released "The Way It Is" in 1986?**

- Bruce Hornsby and the Range
- Bob Seger
- Robbie Nevil
- Richard Marx

**68/ In 1988, who released the #10 bestselling song of the year titled "Roll With It"?**

- Lou Gramm
- Peter Gabriel
- Steve Winwood
- Robert Palmer

**69/ Who released the 1972 song "Sylvia's Mother"?**

- Three Dog Night
- Nilsson
- Chicago
- Dr. Hook & (The Medicine Show)

## 70/ "Hitchin' a Ride" was released in 1969 by what band?

- Vanity Fare
- Herman's Hermits
- Dave Clark Five
- David Bowie

## 71/ In 1971 what group released the song "I'd Like To Teach The World To Sing"?

- The Hillside Singers
- Peter, Paul and Mary
- Maureen McGovern
- The New Seekers

## 72/ In 1988 who released the song titled "Man In The Mirror"?

- Robert Palmer
- Billy Ocean
- Michael Jackson
- Richard Marx

## 73/ Who released the song "Is There Something I Should Know" in 1983?

- Spandau Ballet
- David Bowie
- Duran Duran
- Wham

## 74/ Who released the song "Gypsy's, Tramps & Thieves" in 1971?

- Carly Simon
- Cher
- Aretha Franklin
- Tina Turner

**75/ In 1987, who hit #1 with the cover of the Tommy James and the Shondells song "Mony Mony"?**

- Beach Boys
- Amazulu
- Status Quo
- Billy Idol

**76/ Who released the song "Sweet Child O' Mine" in 1988?**

- Sheryl Crow
- Guns N' Roses
- Def Leppard
- Poison

**77/ Finish the lyrics to the 1987 song "I Wanna Dance With Somebody" - "I wanna dance with somebody, Oh I wanna feel ____ ____ with somebody"**

- the beat
- the heat
- so complete
- the floor

**78/ "Tainted Love" was covered by what band in 1981?**

- Soft Cell
- Gloria Jones
- Tommy Tutone
- Vanilla Ice

**79/ Name the 1970 song released by "Badfinger", then covered by "Harry Nilsson" and "Mariah Carey"?**

- "Without You"
- "Someday"
- "Can't Let Go"
- "I'll Be There"

**80/ In 1985, who released the song "King For A Day?**

- Hall and Oates
- Thompson Twins
- Duran Duran
- Wham

**81/ "Heart Of Glass" was the first #1 single in 1979 for what band?**

- Blondie
- Boomtown Rats
- Police
- Dr. Hook

**82/ Name The Song that has the lyrics - "If you see a faded sign by the side of the road that says 15 miles" (1989)**

- "Rock Lobster"
- "Shake That Cosmic Thing"
- "Love Shack"
- "Roam"

**83/ Name the group who released the song "The Joker" in 1973?**

- Three Dog Night
- Steve Miller Band
- Bachman-Turner Overdrive
- Doobie Brothers

**84/ Who released the song "Tonight's the Night (Gonna Be Alright)" in 1977?**

- Thelma Houston
- The Eagles
- Peter Frampton
- Rod Stewart

**85/ "Do You Really Want To Hurt Me" was released in 1982 by what group?**

- Culture Club
- Duran Duran
- Eurhythmics
- Toni Basil

**86/ Who covered the 1977 song "When I Need You" on their album "Endless Flight"?**

- Eric Carmen
- David Soul
- Leo Sayer
- Albert Hammond

**87/ "Don't Go Breaking My Heart" was released in 1976 by Elton John and who?**

- Dion Warwick
- Kiki Dee
- Jennifer Rush
- Aretha Franklyn

**88/ "She Drives Me Crazy" was released by what group in 1989?**

- Fine Young Cannibals
- Seal
- Mike + the Mechanics
- Great White

**89/ "Miss You Much" was a #1 hit for what female artist in 1989?**

- Janet Jackson
- Paula Abdul
- Debbie Gibson
- Taylor Dayne

**90/ Who covered the song "Delta Dawn" in 1973 taking it to the #14 position for the year?**

- Tanya Tucker
- Bette Midler
- Helen Reddy
- Dianne Davidson

**91/ "Love Will Keep Us Together" was the #1 Billboard Top 100 song for 1975 and was sung by who?**

- The Carpenters
- Melissa Manchester
- Neil Sedaka
- The Captain & Tennille

**92/ "Nothing's Gonna Stop Us Now" was released in 1987 by what group?**

- Jefferson Airplane
- Starship
- George Michael
- Pet Shop Boys

**93/ Who released "Billie Jean" in 1983?**

- Elton John
- Michael Jackson
- Stevie Wonder
- Duran Duran

**94/ What band sang "Can't Fight This Feeling" in 1985?**

- A-Ha
- Starship
- REO Speedwagon
- Tears For Fears

**95/ In 1976, what band released the song "If You Leave Me Now"?**

- Chicago
- Showaddywaddy
- Hot Chocolate
- Boomtown Rats

**96/ Who released the 1979 song "Born To Be Alive"**

- Billy Joel
- George Benson
- Billy Squire
- Patrick Hernandez

**97/ In 1983, who released the song "Total Eclipse Of The Heart"?**

- Juice Newton
- Kim Carnes
- Bonnie Tyler
- Nicki French

**98/ Name the song with the lyrics - "I don't need a whole lot of money. I don't need a big fine car" (Released in 1967 and covered in 1974)**

- "Shinin' On"
- "We're An American Band"
- "Some Kind Of Wonderful"
- "Gimme Shelter"

**99/ Who released the 1986 song "Everybody Have Fun Tonight"?**

- Crowded House
- Whitesnake
- Jody Watley
- Wang Chung

**100/ Name the group that released "Rock The Casbah" in 1982?**

- The Clash
- Slade
- Poison
- Beastie Boys

**101/ Who released the song "Band Of Gold" in 1970?**

- Belinda Carlisle
- Charly McClain
- Freda Payne
- Bonnie Tyler

**102/ "Brass In Pocket" was released in 1979 By who?**

- The Special
- Police
- Pretenders
- Blondie

**103/ What male singer released the song "I'm In You" in 1977?**

- Lionel Richie
- James Taylor
- Peter Frampton
- Stephen Bishop

**104/ Name the song with the lyrics - "Call me good, call me bad. Call me anything you want to baby. (1985)**

- "A Good Heart"
- "Into The Groove"
- "The Power Of Love"
- "I'm Your Man"

**105/ Who covered the song "Lucy In The Sky With Diamonds" in 1975?**

- George Michaels
- The Beatles
- Elton John
- David Bowie

**106/ Who released the song "Reelin' In The Years" in 1973?**

- Curtis Mayfield
- Loggins and Messina
- Doobie Brothers
- Steely Dan

**107/ Finish the lyrics to the 1989 song "Straight Up" by Paula Abdul "Straight up, now tell me do you really wanna love me forever, Oh, oh, oh, or am I caught in ____ ____ ____ ____ "**

- "a game for fun"
- "love me and run"
- "a hit and run"
- "the game you won"

**108/ Complete the first line of the 1989 Guns N' Roses song "Patience" ("___ ___ ___ 'cause I'm missing you")?**

- Shed a tear
- come on home
- my hearts broken
- I'm so lonely

**109/ Who released the #4 song of 1973 called "My Love"?**

- Elton John
- Paul McCartney and Wings
- Marvin Gaye
- Diana Ross

110/ Finish the missing lyric in the 1st verse of the song "Woman" - "Woman, I can hardly ____"?

- Express
- Explain
- Believe
- Wait

111/ In 1977 What band released the song "Cold As Ice"?

- Survivor
- Cheap Trick
- Triumph
- Foreigner

112/ Name the song with the lyrics - "My child arrived just the other day. He came to the world in the usual way" (1974)

- "The Night That The Lights Went Out In Georgia"
- "Cat's In The Cradle"
- "Wildfire"
- "Sara Smile"

113/ Who covered the song "Don't Leave Me This Way" in 1977?

- Harold Melvin and the Blue Notes
- Thelma Houston
- The Communards
- Patty Labelle

114/ What group released the song "Me and You and a Dog Named Boo" in 1971?

- Lobo
- Stampeders
- Chicago
- Looking Glass

**115/ What was the last Elvis Presley song released before his death?**

- Way Down
- My Way
- Burning Love
- In The Ghetto

**116/ "Everything I Own" was released in 1972 by what group?**

- Dramatics
- Bread
- Paul Simon
- Al Green

**117/ Name the song with the lyrics - "When the night falls down, I wait for you, and you come around" (1987)**

- "Eternal Flame"
- "We Got The Beat"
- "Hazy Shade of Winter"
- "Heaven Is A Place On Earth"

**118/ Name the 1979 song with the lyrics "Young Man, there's no need to feel down"?**

- "In The Navy"
- "Y.M.C.A."
- "Macho Man"
- "Go West"

**119/ Who released the 1984 song "Time After Time"?**

- Lionel Richie
- Pointer Sisters
- Deniece Williams
- Cyndi Lauper

**120/ Finish the missing lyric to the 1978 song "Da Ya Think I'm Sexy" - "If you want my body and you think I'm sexy, Come on _____ let me know"?**

- Baby
- Honey
- Sugar
- Darling

**121/ What group released the song "Angie" in 1973?**

- Aerosmith
- Poison
- Tom Petty and the Heartbreakers
- The Rolling Stones

**122/ Name the song with the lyrics "I'm gonna be your number one. Number one" (1980)?**

- "(Just Like) Starting Over"
- "The Tide Is High"
- "Super Trouper"
- "Being With You"

**123/ Name the group who released "Knowing Me, Knowing You" in 1977?**

- Fleetwood Mac
- Abba
- Edison Lighthouse
- The Poppy Family

**124/ "Hangin' Tough" was released in 1989? By what group?**

- Steve Miller  Band
- Queen
- U2
- New Kids On The Block

**125/ Who sang the song in 1987 titled "I Knew You Were Waiting (For Me) with George Michaels?**

- Whitney Houston
- Elton John
- Aretha Franklin
- Boogy Box High

**126/ What group released the 1974 song "Waterloo"?**

- Paper Lace
- Gladys Knight and the Pips
- Abba
- The Carpenters

**127/ Name The Song with the lyrics  - "Midnight, and I'm a waiting on the 12-0-5. Hoping it'll take me just a little farther down the line" (Released in 1979 and covered 1981)**

- "The Sweetest Thing (I've Ever Known)"
- "Angel Of The Morning"
- "Queen of Hearts"
- "Break It to Me Gently"

**128/ Name the band who released the 1971 song "Brown Sugar"?**

- The Beatles
- The Rolling Stones
- Bee Gees
- The Doors

**129/ "Rhythm is Gonna Get You" was released in 1987 by who?**

- Expose
- Belinda Carlisle
- Gloria Estefan and the Miami Sound Machine
- Selena

**130/ What band released the song "Don't You Want Me" in 1981?**

- Police
- Human League
- New Edition
- Wham

**131/ What singer covered the Umberto Tozzi song "Gloria" in 1982?**

- Van Morrison
- Laura Branigan
- Neil Diamond
- Kim Wilde

**132/ "The Living Years" was released in 1988 by what group?**

- Bad English
- Jeff Healey Band
- Mike + the Mechanics
- Huey Lewis & the News

**133/ What male singer released the song "All Those Years Ago" in 1981?**

- George Harrison
- Steely Dan
- Gerry Rafferty
- Dan Fogelberg

**134/ "Cum On Feel The Noize" was originally released in 1973 by what band?**

- Quiet Riot
- Slade
- Animals
- Rolling Stones

## 135/ Who released "(Just Like) Starting Over" in 1980?

- Julian Lennon
- Roxy Music
- Smokey Robinson
- John Lennon

## 136/ The "Sultans of Swing" was released in 1978 by what band?

- Earth Wind and Fire
- The Wings
- Dire Straits
- Little River Band

## 137/ Who released the 1971 song "Draggin' The Line"?

- Tommy James
- Stevie Wonder
- Neil Diamond
- Three Dog Night

## 138/ Who released the song "Dancing on the Ceiling" in 1986?

- Billy Ocean
- Stevie Wonder
- Hall & Oates
- Lionel Richie

## 139/ "Let My Love Open The Door" was released in 1980 by who?

- The Rolling Stones
- The Who
- Peter Gabriel
- Pete Townshend

**140/ The song "Ghostbusters" was released in 1984 by who?**

- Ray Stevens
- Ray Parker Jr.
- Ray Connolly
- Jimmy Ray

**141/ Finish the lyrics to the 1989 song "The Look" by Roxette "Walking like a man, hitting like a hammer, She's a juvenile scam, ____ ____ ____ ____ "**

- "never was a quitter"
- "always was a sinner"
- "strutting with a shimmer"
- "trying to be the winner"

**142/ The #2 bestselling song of 1988 "Need You Tonight" was released in 1987 by who?**

- Cutting Crew
- Rick Astley
- Crowded House
- INXS

**143/ Name the group who had the #1 hit "Down Under" in 1983?**

- UB40
- Kajagoogoo
- Men At Work
- Boys II Men

**144/ Who originally released the song "The Night The Lights Went Out In Georgia" in 1972?**

- Vicki Lawrence
- Reba McEntire
- Carly Simon
- Helen Reddy

**145/ What band released the song "Come On Eileen" in 1983?**

- Dexy's Midnight Runners
- The Jam
- Police
- Culture Club

**146/ Who released the #7 bestselling song of 1989 titled "Wind Beneath My Wings"?**

- Cher
- Taylor Dayne
- Whitney Houston
- Bette Midler

**147/ In the 1989 song "My Prerogative" by Bobby Brown, In the second verse what was his response to the first line "They Say I'm Crazy"?**

- That's my prerogative
- But I don't give a damn
- I really don't care
- Why am I so real

**148/ Finish the missing lyrics from the 1987 George Michael song "Faith" "Oh but I need some time off from that emotion. Time to pick my____ ____ off the floor"**

- "head up"
- "feet up"
- "heart up"
- life up"

**149/ Who released "Open Your Heart" in 1987?**

- Kim Wilde
- Madonna
- Debbie Gibson
- Cher

**150/ Who released the song "Jessie's Girl" in 1981?**

- Rick Springfield
- Hall and Oates
- Foreigner
- Rod Stewart

**151/ Who released the song "Bohemian Rhapsody in 1975?**

- Queen
- ELO (Electric Light Orchestra)
- OMD (Orchestral Manoeuvres In the Dark)
- David Bowie

**152/ In 1973 what group released the song "Tie A Yellow Ribbon 'Round The Ole Oak Tree"?**

- The Isley Brothers
- The Four Seasons
- Tony Orlando and Dawn
- The Spinners

**153/ In 1988, what metal band released the song "Every Rose Has Its Thorn"?**

- Guns 'N Roses
- Poison
- Def Leppard
- ACDC

**154/ What song did Dave Edmunds cover on the album "Rockpile" in 1970?**

- "I Hear You Knocking"
- "Baby I Love You"
- "Born To Be With You"
- "Queen of Hearts"

**155/ What female singer released "Morning Train (Nine to Five)" in 1981?**

- Sheena Easton
- Dolly Parton
- Juice Newton
- Pointer Sisters

**156/ What group released the song "Alive And Kicking" in 1986?**

- Simply Red
- Simple Minds
- Pet Shop Boys
- Glass Tiger

**157/ Who hit #21 on the Billboard charts for 1974 with their version of "Billy Don't Be A Hero"?**

- Paper Lace
- Bo Donaldson and The Heywoods
- Blue Swede
- George McCrae

**158/ Who released the song "Arthur's Theme" in 1982?**

- Michael Murphy
- Hall and Oates
- Christopher Cross
- Sergio Mendes

**159/ Name the song with the lyrics - "Life is a mystery, everyone can stand alone" (1989)**

- "Eternal Flame"
- "Especially For You"
- "Something's Got a Hold of My heart"
- "Like A Prayer"

**160/ Name the artist or group who had the #2 bestselling song of 1987 titled "Alone"?**

-   The Bangles
-   Whitesnake
-   Heart
-   Whitney Houston

**161/ What group released the song "Get Down Tonight" in 1975?**

-   Earth Wind and Fire
-   Grand Funk
-   Ohio Players
-   KC and the Sunshine Band

**162/ Name the artist/group who covered the song "Baby, I Love your Way" in 1989?**

-   Peter Frampton
-   Will to Power
-   Big Mountain
-   Phil Collins

**163/ Who had the #1 hit song in 1984 titled "I Just Called To Say I Love You"?**

-   Lionel Richie
-   Stevie Wonder
-   George Michael
-   Phil Collins

**164 "Party All The Time" was released in 1985 by who?**

-   Eddie Money
-   Robert Palmer
-   Lionel Richie
-   Eddie Murphy

**165/ Who released the #1 bestselling song of 1984 titled "Careless Whisper"?**

- Wham
- Duran Duran
- Foreigner
- Hall and Oates

**166/ Name the group that released "Crazy Little Thing Called Love" in 1979?**

- The Who
- Paul McCartney and Wings
- Air Supply
- Queen

**167/ Who released the song "R.O.C.K. In The U.S.A." in 1985?**

- Bruce Springsteen
- Mike + the Mechanics
- John Mellencamp
- Van Halen

**168/ Who released the song "You Light Up My Life" in 1978?**

- Debby Boone
- Tiffany
- Linda Ronstadt
- Kylie Minogue

**169/ What group released the 1973 song "Takin' Care Of Business"?**

- The Guess Who
- Bachman-Turner Overdrive
- War
- Earth Wind and Fire

**170/ Name The Song with the lyrics - "Jeremiah was a bullfrog, was a good friend of mine. I never understood a single word he said, but I helped him a-drink his wine" (1970)**

- "Jeremiah Was a Bullfrog"
- "Signs"
- "Joy To The World"
- "Friends and Lovers"

**171/ In 1986, who released the song "Rock Me Amadeus"?**

- Zagar and Evans
- Berlin
- Falco
- Glen Medeiros

**172/ Name the singer or group that released the song titled "The Long Run" in 1979?**

- The Eagles
- Billy Joel
- Nitty Gritty Dirt Band
- Rod Stewart

**173/ Who released the song titled "Neutron Dance" in 1984?**

- Aretha Franklin
- Pointer Sisters
- Whitney Houston
- Diana Ross

**174/ The song "Call Me" was released in 1980 by what band?**

- The Knack
- Dr. Hook
- Blondie
- The Pretenders

175/ Name the singer who took "Ricky Don't Lose That Number" to #51 in 1974?

- Rufus
- Johnny Bristol
- Todd Rundgren
- Steely Dan

176/ Who released the 1973 song "Sunshine On My Shoulders"?

- Jim Croce
- John Denver
- James Taylor
- Glen Campbell

177/ "Things Can Only Get Better" was released in 1985 by who?

- Howard Jones
- Duran Duran
- Crowded House
- Huey Lewis and the News

178/ "Hit Me With Your Best Shot" was released in 1980 By what female singer?

- Bonnie Tyler
- Sheena Easton
- Gloria Gaynor
- Pat Benatar

179/ The song "Church Of The Poison Mind" was released in 1983 by what group?

- Tears For Fears
- A-Ha
- Culture Club
- Dire Straits

**180/ The song "Celebration" was released in 1980 by who?**

- Earth Wind and Fire
- KC and the Sunshine Band
- Kool and the Gang
- Billy Squire

**181/ Name the song with the lyrics - "When you're weary, feeling small. When tears are in your eyes, I will dry them all" (1970)**

- "The Sounds Of Silence"
- "Mrs. Robinson"
- "Homeward Bound"
- "Bridge Over Troubled Water"

**182/ According to the 1972 song "My Ding-A-Ling", who bought him a cute little toy?**

- Grandpa
- Mommy
- Grandma
- Papa

**183/ In the 1985 Dire Straits song "Money for Nothing" what is it they say was free in the line "Money for Nothing and the _____ for free"?**

- Chips
- Chicks
- Tips
- Shirts

**184/ Name the artist who released the #1 song "Papa Don't Preach" in 1986?**

- Whitney Houston
- Diana Ross
- Madonna
- Kylie Minogue

**185/ In 1979, who released the song "We Don't Talk Anymore"?**

- Cliff Richard
- Johnny Logan
- David  Bowie
- Olivia Newton John

**186/ Footloose was released in 1984 by what singer?**

- Eddie Rabbitt
- Ray Parker Jr.
- Kenny Loggins
- Corey Hart

**187/ Name the song with the lyrics - "I don't want to talk, about things we've gone through. Though it's hurting me now it's history" (1980)**

- "The Winner Takes It All"
- "Crying"
- "The Tide Is High"
- "Woman In Love"

**188/ Who had the #1 song in 1978 titled "Three Times A Lady"?**

- Lionel Richie
- Bee Gees
- David Soul
- The Commodores

**189/ What group released the song "Rock And Roll All Nite" in 1975?**

- Peter Frampton
- Bay City Rollers
- Kiss
- Steve Miller Band

**190/ "Say You Say Me" was released in 1986 by who?**

- Lionel Richie
- Billy Ocean
- Michael McDonald
- The Commodores

**191/ Name the group who released the 1976 song "You Sexy Thing"?**

- Silver Connection
- Hot Chocolate
- War
- Ohio Players

**192/ Name the song with the lyrics - "Funny how it seems, always in time, but never in line for dreams". (1983)?**

- "Is There Something I Should Know"
- "Baby Jane"
- "Hello"
- "True"

**193/ Who released the song "Spiders And Snakes" in 1973?**

- Jim Stafford
- Ray Stevens
- Mac Davis
- Al Wilson

**194/ Who covered the song "Greatest Love Of All" making it the #11 bestselling song of 1986?**

- Dionne Warwick
- Whitney Houston
- Abba
- George Benson

**195/ What Band released "Look Away in 1988?**

- Mike + the Mechanics
- Chicago
- Jeff Healey Band
- Van Halen

**196/ Name the song with the lyrics - "Promise me son, not to do the things I've done. Walk away from trouble if you can" (1980)**

- "The Special"
- "Coward of the County"
- "Working My Way Back To You"
- "Stand and Deliver"

**197/ What group released the song "I'll Take You There" in 1972?**

- The Hollies
- Carly Simon
- Gladys Knight and the Pips
- The Staple Singers

**198/ Name the Actor who had the hit song in 1977 titled "Don't Give Up On Us"?**

- Ricky Gervais
- David Soul
- Cheryl Ladd
- Eddie Murphy

**199/ Who covered the 1968 song "Red Red Wine" hitting the #1 position in 1983?**

- Neil Diamond
- UB40
- Feargal Sharkey
- Jim Diamond

**200/ The song "Sara Smile" was the #11 song for 1976 and was sung by who?**

- Hall & Oates
- Silver Connection
- Paul Simon
- Starship

**201/ What Group released the song "25 Or 6 To 4" in 1970?**

- Santana
- Chicago
- The Guess Who
- Brotherhood of Man

**202/ Name the #1 hit song from 1970 with the lyrics "When no-one else can understand me. When everything I do is wrong"?**

- "Tears of a Clown"
- "Band of Gold"
- "Get It On"
- "The Wonder of You"

**203/ Who released the 1981 song "Chariots Of Fire"?**

- Zager and Evans
- Asia
- Vangelis
- OMD (Orchestral Manoeuvres In The Dark)

**204/ Who released the song "If You Don't Know Me By Now" in 1972?**

- Harold Melvin & the Blue Notes
- Simply Red
- Richard Marx
- Chicago

**205/ Who released the song titled "Out Of Touch" in 1984?**

- Hall and Oates
- Thomson Twins
- Lionel Richie
- Tears For Fears

**206/ In 1970, who released the song called "In The Summertime"?**

- Smokey Robinson
- Rod Stewart
- Mungo Jerry
- Clive Dunn

**207/ What female singer released the song "You're So Vain" in 1972?**

- Carly Simon
- Melissa Manchester
- Roberta Flack
- Helen Reddy

**208/ Name the song with the lyrics - "First I was afraid I was petrified. Kept thinking I could never live without you by my side" (1978)**

- "Hit Me With Your Best Shot"
- "I Will Survive"
- "Ring My Bell"
- "Call Me"

**209/ Name the Song with the lyrics - "I never seen you looking so lovely as you did tonight? (1986)**

- "I Want To Wake Up With You"
- "Take My Breath Away"
- "Lady In Red"
- "La Isla Bonita"

# TOP 100 HITS 70's & 80's ANSWERS

**1/ Finish the lyrics from the 1985 Mr. Mister song "Broken Wings" - "Take these broken wings and learn to fly again,____ ____ ____ ____ ____ "**

Answer: "learn to live so free" (The Mr. Mister song was the #5 bestselling song of the year and released from their "Welcome to the Real World" album)

**2/ What 1966 Supremes hit did Phil Collins cover in 1982?**

Answer: "You Can't Hurry Love"    ("You Can't Hurry Love" spent 2 weeks at #1 in the UK and was the #37 bestselling song of 1983 in the U.S. It was released from his album "Hello, I Must Be Going!")

**3/ Who released the song "He ain't Heavy, He's My Brother" in 1969?**

Answer: The Hollies (The Hollies spent 2 weeks at #1 in the UK in 1968 and became the #46 bestselling song of 1970 in the U.S. It was released as a single with "Cos You Like To Love" as the B-side)

**4/ Name the Song with the lyrics "The first time ever I saw your face. I thought the sun rose in your eyes, and the moon and stars were the gifts you gave" (1972)**

Answer: -    "The First Time Ever I Saw Your Face" (Released from Roberta Flacks album "First Take". The song has been covered at least 39 times since 1972)

**5/ Who had a #1 hit and #26 bestselling song of 1989 titled "Blame It On The Rain"?**

Answer: Milli Vanilli  (Milli Vanilli released this song from their "Girl You Know It's True" album)

**6/ In 1983 what band released "Talking In Your Sleep"?**

Answer: The Romantics (The Romantics released this song from their album "In Heat" becoming the #19 song of 1984)

**7/ What artist released "Never Gonna Give You Up" in 1987 becoming the #4 bestselling song of the year in the U.S.?**

Answer: Rick Astley (Rick Astley released the song from his album "Whenever You Need Somebody")

**8/ Who covered the 1988 song "Girl You Know It's True"?**

Answer: Milli Vanilli          (The song became the #8 song of 1989 and was originally released by a band called Numarx in 1977)

**9/ Who released the 1972 song "Schools Out"?**

Answer: Alice Cooper ("Schools Out" spent 3 weeks at #1 in the UK and peaked at #7 in the U.S.)

**10/ What group released "Eternal Flame" in 1989?**

Answer: The Bangles ("Eternal Flame" spent 4 weeks at #1 in the UK and 1 week in the U.S. in Apr. 1989. It was released from their album titled "Everything")

**11/ What band released "Don't You (Forget About Me)" in 1982?**

Answer: Simple Minds (Simple Minds released the song from "The Breakfast Club" soundtrack)

**12/ What group released the song "Give A Little Bit" in 1977?**

Answer: Supertramp (Released from their album "Even In The Quietest Moments", the song peaked at #15 on the Billboard Pop Singles chart)

**13/ Finish the lyrics to the 1986 song "Lady in red, is dancing with me ___ ___ ___ "**

Answer: "cheek to cheek" (In Aug 1986, Chris DeBurgh spent 3 consecutive weeks at #1 in the U.K with the song "Lady In Red" and became the #21 bestselling song of 1987 in the U.S.)

**14/ Who released the song "Rocket Man" in 1972?**

Answer: Elton John (Elton John released the song from his album "Honky Chateau")

**15/ What male singer released the song "Superstition" in 1973?**

Answer: Stevie Wonder (Stevie Wonder hit the #1 position in the U.S. and was released from his album "Talking Book")

**16/ Who had the #40 song of 1970 titled "Love Grows (Where my Rosemary Goes)"?**

Answer: Edison Lighthouse (Sung by studio session singer Tony Burrows, the song raced to #1 in the UK. A group called the "Greefields" were brought in to lip sync to the song on the UK TV-show "Top of the Pops" under the name Edison Lighthouse.)

**17/ In 1976, who released the song "Saturday Night"?**

Answers: Bay City Rollers (This was the only #1 hit in the U.S. for the Bay City Rollers however they had 10 top 10 hits in the U.K. "Saturday Night" was never released as a U.K. single)

**18/ Name the song with the lyrics - "Watching every motion in my foolish lover's game. On this endless ocean finally lovers know no shame" (1986)**

- " Answer: "Take My Breath Away" ("Take My Breath Away" was used in the film "Top Gun" and performed by Berlin. It became the #27 bestselling song of 1986 in the U.S.)

**19/ What band released the song "Layla" in 1971?**

Answer: Derek and the Dominos ("Layla and other Assorted Love Songs" Eric Clapton played with the band.)

**20/ Who had the hit song "Only In My Dreams" in 1987?**

Answer: Debbie Gibson ("Only In My Dreams" was Gibson's debut single from her album "Out Of The Blue". It became the #26 bestselling song of the year)

**21/ Who released the song "Our Lips Are Sealed" in 1981?**

Answer: The Go-Go's (The Go-Go's released "Our Lips are Sealed" from their album "Beauty and the Beast" peaking at #20. The Fun Boy Three version in 1983 hit #7 in the U.K.)

**22/ The song "Hello" was released in 1984 by who?**

Answer: Lionel Richie (Lionel Richie spent 6 consecutive weeks at #1 in the UK and was the #7 song of the year in the U.S. It was released from his "Can't Slow Down" album)

**23/ Name the group who had the 1987 hit song title "Notorious"?**

Answer: Duran Duran (This was the title track from their album and it peaked at #2 in the U.S.)

**24/ "December 1963 (Oh, What a Night)" was released in 1975 by what group?**

Answer: The Four Seasons (The Four Seasons spent 3 weeks at #1 in the U.S. in Mar. 1976 and was released from their album "Who Loves You)

**25/ Who sung the #2 song for 1974 titled "Seasons In The Sun"?**

Answer: Terry Jacks (This song was originally released by the co-writer Jacques Brel in 1961 before the Terry Jacks single release in 1973)

**26/ Name the song with the lyrics - "Last night I dreamt of San Pedro, just like I'd never gone, I new the song" (1987)**

Answer: "La Isla Bonita" ("La Isla Bonita" spent 2 weeks at #1 in the UK becoming her 4th #1 single and the most by a female artist in the UK at that time. It peaked at #4 on the Billboard Hot 100 Charts in the U.S.)

**27/ What singer/group released the #12 song for 1989 titled "Waiting For A Star To Fall"?**

Answer: Boy Meets Girl (Boy Meets Girl released it from their album "Reel Life")

**28/ What is it that is multiplyin' in the 1978 song "You're The One That I Want"?**

Answer: Chills (Released from the "Grease" soundtrack, the song spent 9 consecutive weeks at #1 in the UK and 1 week in the U.S. It hit the top spot in 13 different countries.)

**29/ Who released "One Night In Bangkok" in 1984?**

Answer: Murray Head (The song was written by ABBA members Benny Andersson & Björn Ulvaeus. It was released from the musical album "Chess" OST )

**30/ In 1986, Gregory Abbott released what #1 hit song? (It reached #3 for Bestselling songs of 1987)**

Answer: "Shake You Down" ("Shake You Down" was the title song from this debut album and his biggest selling recording) hitting #1 in the U.S. & #6 in the U.K)

**31/ What band released "Owner of a Lonely Heart" in 1983?**

Answer: Yes (Yes, released this song from their album "90125" which became the #8 song of 1984)

**32/ Who released the song "Clap For The Wolfman" in 1974?**

Answer: The Guess Who (The Guess Who released "Clap For The Wolfman" from their album "Road Food" with Burton Cummings on lead vocals)

**33/ What band released "Never Can Say Goodbye" in 1971?**

Answer: Jackson Five ("Never Can Say Goodbye" was covered by Gloria Gaynor in 1974 and communards in 1977)

**34/ Who had the Number 1 song for 1978 called "Shadow Dancing"?**

Answer: Andy Gibb (This was the title song from his album and was backed up by his brothers group "The Bee Gees".)

**35/ What band released the song "Signs" in 1971?**

Answer: Five Man Electrical Band (Originally released as a "B" side song in 1970. The unsuccessful A-side was "Hello Melinda Goodbye")

**36/ Who released the song "When Doves Cry" in 1984?**

Answer: Prince ("When Doves Cry became the top selling single of 1984 and was release from the Prince album "Purple Rain")

**37/ Name the song with the lyrics - "Hey, once I was a funky singer, playin' in a Rock and Roll Band. I never had no problem" (1976)**

Answer: -    "Play That Funky Music" ("Play That Funky Music" was the #5 song of 1976 and was released from their self-titled album "Wild Cherry")

**38/ Who released "Another Brick In The Wall" in 1979?**

Answer: Pink Floyd ("Another Brick In The Wall" became the #2 bestselling song of 1979 in the U.S. and spent 5 consecutive weeks at #1 in the UK. It was released from the Pink Floyd album "The Wall")

**39/ In 1971 who released the song "Brand New Key"?**

Answer: Melanie (Melanie Safka wrote and released the #1 song from her album "Gather Me")

**40/ What Duet released the song "Leather And Lace" in 1981?**

Answer: Stevie Nicks and Don Henley (Stevie Nicks was asked by Waylon Jennings and Jessi Colter to write the title track for their album Leather and Lace. Stevie Nicks teamed up with Don Henley to record the song from Stevie Nicks "Bella Donna" album)

**41/ What female singer released "Self Control" in 1984?**

Answer: Laura Branigan (Laura Branigan released this as the title track from her album peaking at #4 in the U.S. but hitting #1 in Canada, Germany and Austria)

**42/ Which Band covered Roy Orbison's song "Oh Pretty Woman" in 1982?**

Answer: Van Halen (From their 1982 album "Driver Down" the song peaked at #12 on the Billboard charts.)

**43/ Name the song with the lyrics - "All the old pain'tings on the tombs, they do the sand dance don't you know" (1986)**

Answer: "Walk Like An Egyptian" (The Bangles had the #1 bestselling song of 1987 with "Walk Like An Egyptian" and it was released from their album "Different Light")

**44/ Name the singer/group who released the song "I'll Be There For You" in 1989?**

Answer: Bon Jovi (The #1 hit song was written and recorded by Bon Jovi and released from their album "New Jersey")

**45/ In 1985, who released the song "Part-Time Lover"?**

Answer: Stevie Wonder (Stevie Wonder released this song from his "In Square Circle" album hitting #1 on 4 Billboard Charts Hot 100, R&B, Dance and Adult Contemporary)

**46/ Name the group who released the song "Hungry Like The Wolf" in 1983?**

Answer: Duran Duran ("Hungry Like The Wolf" became the #17 song of 1983 and was released from their album "Rio")

**47/ What group released the song "I Still Haven't Found What I'm looking For" in 1987?**

Answer: U2 (This #1 single was released from their album "The Joshua Tree" becoming the #23 song of 1987)

**48/ What group released "Funkytown" in 1980?**

Answer: Lipps Inc (Lipps Inc released the song from their "Mouth to Mouth" album becoming the #8 song of 1980. It was covered by Pseudo Echo in 1986)

**49/ Name the song with the lyrics - "I can think of younger days, when living for my life was everything a man could want to do" ( 1971)**

Answer: "How Can You Mend A Broken Heart" ("How Can You Mend A Broken Heart" Hit #1 in Canada and the U.S. and peaked at #3 in Australia. It was released from the Bee Gees "Trafalgar album with "Country Woman" as the B-side of the single)

**50/ How many times did Tony Orlando want to knock on the pipe in his 1971 song "Knock Three Times"?**

Answer: Twice (The lyric was "Oh my darling, knock three times on the ceiling if you want me, Mmm Mmm, twice on the pipe")

**51/ Name The Song with the lyrics - "I Have a picture pinned to my wall. An image of you and me and we're laughing and loving it all" ( 1983)**

Answer: "Hold Me Now" ("Hold Me Now" was released by the Thomson Twins from their album "into The Gap" and peaked at #3 on the Billboard charts)

**52/ What 1962 Roy Orbison song did Don McLean cover in 1980?**

Answer: "Crying" ("Crying" spent 3 weeks at #1 in the UK and was the #40 song of 1980 In the U.S. It was released from his 1978 album "Chain Lightning")

**53/ "Spirit In The Sky" was released by who in 1969?**

Answer: Norman Greenbaum (The song spent 2 weeks at #1 in the UK and Peaked at #3 on the U.S. Billboard charts. It was covered in 1986 by Doctor and the Medics)

**54/ Name The Song with the lyrics - "What I want, you've got, and it might be hard to handle. But like the flame that burns the candle. The candle feeds the flame" (1981)**

Answer: "You Make My Dreams" (Topping the charts at #5 "You Make My Dreams" was released from the Hall & Oates album "Voices")

**55/ "Holding Back the Years" was released in 1982 by "The Frantic Elevators" The band re-released the song in 1985 under what name?**

Answer: Simply Red: (Simply Red hit #1 with the song in July 1986 and was released from their album "Picture Book")

**56/ In 1979 what male singer released the song "Cars"?**

Answer: Gary Numan (The song peaked at #9 in the U.S. but spent 2 weeks at #1 in Canada and 1 week at the top of the charts in the UK. It was released from "The Pleasure Principle" album)

**57/ Who covered the song "Saving All My Love For You" in 1985?**

Answer: Whitney Houston (The song was originally released in 1978 by Marilyn McCoo & Billy Davis Jr. before the Whitney Houston cover spent 2 weeks at #1 in the U.K and became the #23 song of the year in the U.S.)

**58/ Name the song with the lyrics - "Kissing like a bandit, Stealing time, Underneath a sycamore tree" (1988)**

Answer: "Wishing Well" (This song became the #12 song of 1988 for Terence Trent D'Arby. It topped both the Billboard Hot 100 and the Soul charts in May 1988 and was featured in the film "Grand Theft Auto IV")

**59/ Who covered the song "Always On My Mind" in 1987?**

Answer: Pet Shop Boys (Released from their album "Introspective" Song made popular by Elvis Presley in 1972 and Willie Nelson 1982 )

**60/ Name the song with the lyrics - "Sleight of hand and twist of fate, on a bed of nails she makes me wait" (1987)**

Answer: "With Or Without You" (The song became the first hit for U2 where it topped the charts in Ireland, Canada and U.S. It was released from their "Joshua Tree" album)

**61/ What male artist released the song "Little Red Corvette" in 1983?**

Answer: Prince (Prince released this song from his album titled "1999")

**62/ Who released the song titled "Space Oddity" in 1972?**

Answer: David Bowie (The songs original release in 1969 reached #5 in UK and #124 in the U.S. The 1972 release in U.S. went to #5 and the 1975 release in the UK spent 2 weeks at #1

**63/ Name The Song with the lyrics - "A long, long time ago, I can still remember how that music used to make me smile" (Released in 1971 & covered in 1999)**

Answer: "American Pie" ("American Pie" was released by Don MacLean and written to commemorate "The Day The Music Died" with the death of Buddy Holly, Ritchie Valens and The Big Bopper in 1959. The song was covered by Madonna in 1999)

**64/ What band released the song "I Want To Know What Love Is" in 1984?**

Answer: Foreigner (Foreigner released the song from their album "Agent Provocateur" becoming the #3 bestselling song of 1985)

**65/ In the 1989 song "Stand" by R.E.M., In the first line, where do they tell you to stand?**

Answer: Stand in the place where you live (This song was the #76 song of 1989 and released from their album "Green" with "Memphis Train Blues" as the B-side)

**66/ The song "(They Long To Be) Close To You" was the #2 song for 1970 was sung by who?**

Answer: The Carpenters: (This was the title song on the album and remained at #1 for 4 consecutive weeks)

**67/ Who wrote and released "The Way It Is" in 1986?**

Answer: Bruce Hornsby and the Range (Bruce Hornsby and the Range (It was the title track from their album and became the #8 bestselling song of 1987)

**68/ In 1988, who released the #10 bestselling song of the year titled "Roll With It"?**

Answer: Steve Winwood (The song spent 4 weeks at #1. It was the title track from his album with "The Morning Side" as the B-side of the single)

**69/ Who released the 1972 song "Sylvia's Mother"?**

Answer: Dr. Hook & (The Medicine Show) (Released from their self-titled album hitting #1 in Ireland and Australia, #2 in the U.K. and #5 in the U.S. The song has been covered by Bon Jovi on his album "This Left Feels Right Live")

**70/ "Hitchin' a Ride" was released in 1969 by what band?**

Answer: Vanity Fare (Vanity Fare released this song as a single with "Man Child" as the B-side)

**71/ In 1971 what group released the song "I'd Like To Teach The World To Sing"?**

Answer: The New Seekers (The New Seekers actually sung the jingle for the Coca Cola commercial. The Hillside singers changed the chorus and both groups had a hit in 1971)

**72/ In 1988 who released the song titled "Man In The Mirror"?**

Answer: Michael Jackson (Released from his album titled "Bad", the song hit #1 in the U.S. and #8 in the U.K. After his death in 1988, it re-entered the U.K. charts and hit #2)

**73/ Who released the song "Is There Something I Should Know" in 1983?**

Answer: Duran Duran (Duran Duran released the song as a standalone single. It spent 2 weeks at #1 in the UK and became the #55 bestselling song of 1983 in the U.S.)

**74/ Who released the song "Gypsy's, Tramps & Thieves" in 1971?**

Answer: Cher (This was the title song from her seventh album with "He'll Never Know" as the B-side. It hit #1 in the U.S. and Canada and top 10 in many other countries)

**75/ In 1987, who hit #1 with the cover of the Tommy James and the Shondells song "Mony Mony"?**

Answer: Billy Idol (All 4 covered the song but it was the Billy Idol live version that replaced another Tommy James cover "I Think We're Alone Now" by Tiffany from the #1 position)

**76/ Who released the song "Sweet Child O' Mine" in 1988?**

Answer: Guns N' Roses (Released from their album "Appetite for Destruction" Sheryl Crow covered the song in 1999. This version was the #5 song of 1988)

**77/ Finish the lyrics to the 1987 song "I Wanna Dance With Somebody" - "I wanna dance with somebody, Oh I wanna feel _____ _____ with somebody"**

Answer: The Heat (Whitney Houston spent 2 weeks at #1 in June 1987 in the UK. The song became the #4 bestselling song of 1987 in the U.S.)

**78/ "Tainted Love" was covered by what band in 1981?**

Answer: Soft Cell ("Tainted Love" was the #11 song of 1981 in the U.S. and spent 2 weeks at #1 in the UK. It was originally released in 1964 by Gloria Jones )

**79/ Name the 1970 song released by "Badfinger", then covered by "Harry Nilsson" and "Mariah Carey"?**

Answer: "Without You" ("Without You" spent 5 weeks at # 1 in 1972 by Nilsson. It was originally released by Badfinger in 1970, Harry Nilsson in 1972 and Mariah Carey in 94)

**80/ In 1985, who released the song "King For A Day?**

Answer: Thompson Twins (The Thompson Twins released the song from their album "Here's to Future Days")

**81/ "Heart Of Glass" was the first #1 single in 1979 for what band?**

Answer: Blondie (This was 1 of 6 songs released from Blondie's album Parallel Lines)

**82/ Name The Song that has the lyrics - "If you see a faded sign by the side of the road that says 15 miles" (1989)**

Answer: "Love Shack" (This was the bands first Million selling record which peaked at #3 on the Billboard charts.)

**83/ Name the group who released the song "The Joker" in 1973?**

Answer: Steve Miller Band (The song hit #1 in the U.S. in 1974 and then was featured in a Levi's commercial in 1990 in the UK (16 years later), where it was re-released and hit #1 in the U.K. and other countries)

**84/ Who released the song "Tonight's the Night (Gonna Be Alright)" in 1977?**

Answer: Rod Stewart (Released from his album "A Night On The Town" the song "Tonight's the Night" became the #1 song of 1977)

**85/ "Do You Really Want To Hurt Me" was released in 1982 by what group?**

Answer: Culture Club (Culture Club released the song from their album "Kissing To Be Clever" and became the #11 song of 1983)

**86/ Who covered the 1977 song "When I Need You" on their album "Endless Flight"?**

Answer: Leo Sayer (The song was originally released by the writer Albert Hammond in 1976 before Leo Sayer spent 3 weeks at #1 in Feb 1977 in the UK and 1 week in the US at the top spot.)

**87/ "Don't Go Breaking My Heart" was released in 1976 by Elton John and who?**

Answer: Kiki Dee (Elton John and Kiki Dee released as a single, then added later to his Greatest Hits album. The single spent 6 consecutive weeks at #1 in the UK and 4 weeks in the U.S.)

**88/ "She Drives Me Crazy" was released by what group in 1989?**

Answer: Fine Young Cannibals (This song was Hit #1 in the U.S. becoming the 18th bestselling song of 1989. It was released from "The Raw and the Cooked" album)

**89/ "Miss You Much" was a #1 hit for what female artist in 1989?**

Answer: Janet Jackson (Janet Jackson released the song on her "Rhythm Nation 1814" album)

**90/ Who covered the song "Delta Dawn" in 1973 taking it to the #14 position for the year?**

Answer: Helen Reddy (Tanya Tucker released the song in 1972 and hit #9 on the Country Charts, Dianne Davidson covered the song that same year while Helen Ready and Bette Midler were set to release the song at the same time in 1973)

**91/ "Love Will Keep Us Together" was the #1 Billboard Top 100 song for 1975 and was sung by who?**

Answer: The Captain & Tennille  (Originally released by the co-writer Neil Sedaka in 1973 on his album "The Tra-La Days are Over". This was the #1 song of 1975)

**92/ "Nothing's Gonna Stop Us Now" was released in 1987 by what group?**

Answer: Starship (Starship released the song from their album "No Protection". This became the #5 bestselling song of 1987. It spent 4 consecutive weeks at #1 in the UK)

**93/ Who released "Billie Jean" in 1983?**

Answer: Michael Jackson ("Billie Jean" managed to hit the top spot in the UK for 1 week only but had more success in the U.S. where it was the #2 highest selling song of the year 1983)

**94/ What band sang "Can't Fight This Feeling" in 1985?**

Answer: REO Speedwagon (REO Speedwagon Released the song from their "Wheels Are Turnin'" album becoming the #13 song of 1985)

**95/ In 1976, what band released the song "If You Leave Me Now"?**

Answer: Chicago (The song spent 3 weeks at #1 in the UK and 2 weeks on the Billboard charts becoming the bands first #1 hit)

**96/ Who released the 1979 song "Born To Be Alive"**

Answer: Patrick Hernandez (The song was #1 on Hot Dance Play charts and sold over 11 Million copies worldwide)

**97/ In 1983, who released the song "Total Eclipse Of The Heart"?**

Answer: Bonnie Tyler (Bonnie Tyler released this on her album "Faster Than The Speed Of Night". Nicki French covered the song in 1994)

**98/ Name the song with the lyrics - "I don't need a whole lot of money. I don't need a big fine car" (Released in 1967 and covered in 1974)**

Answer: "Some Kind Of Wonderful" ("Some Kind Of Wonderful" was released from the Grand Funk Railroad album, "All the Girls in the World  Beware!!!" hitting the #1 spot in the U.S.)

**99/ Who released the 1986 song "Everybody Have Fun Tonight"?**

Answer: Wang Chung (Released from their album "Mosaic" the song peaked at #2 on the Billboard Hot 100. It became the #12 song of 1987)

**100/ Name the group that released "Rock The Casbah" in 1982?**

Answer: (The #52 song of 1983 by The Clash was from their album titled "Combat Rock")

**101/ Who released the song "Band Of Gold" in 1970?**

Answer: Freda Payne (The other 3 artists recorded the song for their albums after the Freda Payne release in 1970)

**102/ "Brass In Pocket" was released in 1979 By who?**

Answer: Pretenders (The Pretenders spent 2 weeks at #1 in the UK and became the #41 song of the year 1979 in the U.S. It was released on their self-titled album)

**103/ What male singer released the song "I'm In You" in 1977?**

Answer: Peter Frampton (It was the title song for his album and hit #2 becoming his most successful record in the U.S.)

**104/ Name the song with the lyrics  - "Call me good, call me bad. Call me anything you want to baby. (1985)**

Answer: "I'm Your Man ("I'm Your Man" spent 2 weeks at #1 in the U.K. and managed the #63 bestselling song of 1985 in the U.S.)

**105/ Who covered the song "Lucy In The Sky With Diamonds" in 1975?**

Answer: Elton John (The original Beatles version was released in 1969. John Lennon participated on the Elton John version with backup vocals and guitar.)

**106/ Who released the song "Reelin' In The Years" in 1973?**

Answer: Steely Dan (Steely Dan Released this from his album "Can't Buy a Thrill" as a single with "Only a Fool Would Say That" as the B-side)

**107/ Finish the lyrics to the 1989 song "Straight Up" by Paula Abdul "Straight up, now tell me do you really wanna love me forever, Oh, oh, oh, or am I caught in ____ ____ ____ ____"**

Answer: "A Hit and Run" (Paula Abdul released the song from her album "Forever Your Girl" becoming the #4 bestselling song of 1989))

**108/ Complete the first line of the 1989 Guns N' Roses song "Patience" ("___ ___ ___ 'cause I'm missing you")?**

Answer: Shed a tear (This song was shot in a single session using 3 acoustic guitars and was released from their "G N' R Lies" album)

**109/ Who released the #4 song of 1973 called "My Love"?**

Answer: Paul McCartney and Wings ("My Love" topped the charts in the U.S. and was released from their album "Red Rose Speedway")

**110/ Finish the missing lyric in the 1st verse of the song "Woman" - "Woman, I can hardly ____"?**

Answer: Express (John Lennon spent 2 weeks at #1 in the UK and the #21 song of 1981 in the U.S.)

**111/ In 1977 What band released the song "Cold As Ice"?**

Answer: Foreigner ("Cold as Ice" was released from their self-titled album originally as the B-side to "Feels Like the First Time" peaking at #6 on the U.S. Pop charts)

**112/ Name the song with the lyrics - "My child arrived just the other day. He came to the world in the usual way" (1974)**

Answer: "Cat's In The Cradle" ("Cat's In the Cradle" was released as a single by Harry Chapin with "Vacancy" as the B-side)

**113/ Who covered the song "Don't Leave Me This Way" in 1977?**

Answer: Thelma Houston (The Harold Melvin version was in 1975 and The communards covered the song again in 1986)

**114/ What group released the song "Me and You and a Dog Named Boo" in 1971?**

Lobo (The song peaked at #5 on the Billboard charts was originally released as a single then added to his debut album "Introducing Lobo")

**115/ What was the last Elvis Presley song released before his death?**

Answer: Way Down ("Way Down" was released June 1977 working it's way up the charts before Elvis died on Aug 16, 1977. It spent 5 weeks at #1 in the UK and peaked at #18 on the Billboard Hot 100. It sold enough copies to become the #64 song of 1977 in the U.S.)

**116/ "Everything I Own" was released in 1972 by what group?**

Answer: Bread (The Bread version peaked at #5 while the cover by Ken Boothe hit #1 for 3 weeks in the U.K. in 1974. It was also covered by Olivia Newton-John, Boy George, NSYNC and Rod Stewart)

**117/ Name the song with the lyrics - "When the night falls down, I wait for you, and you come around" (1987)**

Answer: "Heaven Is A Place On Earth" ("Heaven Is A Place On Earth" hit #1 Dec. 1987 and became the #7 bestselling song of 1988.)

**118/ Name the 1979 song with the lyrics "Young Man, there's no need to feel down"?**

Answer: "Y.M.C.A." ("Y.M.C.A. became the #8 bestselling song of 1979 in the U.S. but peaked at #2 on the charts. It hit #1 in several countries and spent 3 weeks at #1 in the UK.)

**119/ Who released the 1984 song "Time After Time"?**

Answer? Cyndi Lauper (Cyndi Lauper wrote and released the song from her album "She's So Unusual" hitting #1 on June 9, 1984)

**120/ Finish the missing lyric to the 1978 song "Da Ya Think I'm Sexy" - "If you want my body and you think I'm sexy, Come on ____ let me know"?**

Answer: Sugar (The song hit #1 in the UK, US and Australia. Rod Stewart donated all of the royalties from the song to Unicef after a plagiarism law suit was filed against him for copying the melody of the 1972 song "Taj Mahal")

**121/ What group released the song "Angie" in 1973?**

Answer: The Rolling Stones (The song was released from their album "Goats Head Soup" and hit #1 in the Billboard Hot 100 and Australia)

**122/ Name the song with the lyrics "I'm gonna be your number one. Number one" (1980)?**

Answer: "The Tide Is High" (Blondie had the #17 song of 1980 and spent 2 weeks at #1 in the UK Nov. 1980)

**123/ Name the group who released "Knowing Me, Knowing You" in 1977?**

Answer:  (The song was released from their album "Arrival")

**124/ "Hangin' Tough" was released in 1989? By what group?**

Answer: New Kids On The Block (New Kids On The Block used this as the title track from their  album. It spent 2 weeks at #1 in the UK Jan 1990)

**125/ Who sang the song in 1987 titled "I Knew You Were Waiting (For Me) with George Michaels?**

Answer: Aretha Franklin ("I Knew You Were Waiting (For Me)" was released from Aretha Franklin's album "Aretha" spending 2 weeks at #1 in the UK and Was the #36 bestselling song of 1987 in the U.S.)

**126/ What group released the 1974 song "Waterloo"?**

Answer: Abba (They won the Eurovision Song Contest with the song in 1974)

**127/ Name The Song with the lyrics  - "Midnight, and I'm a waiting on the 12-0-5. Hoping it'll take me just a little farther down the line" (Released in 1979 and covered 1981)**

Answer: "Queen Of Hearts" (The song peaked at #2 in the U.S. but was the #14 song of 1981 for Juice Newton. It was released from her album "Juice")

**128/ Name the band who released the 1971 song "Brown Sugar"?**

Answer: The Rolling Stones ("Brown Sugar spent 2 weeks at #1 on the Billboard charts in the U.S. and was released from their album "Sticky fingers" with "Bitch" as the B-side of their single)

**129/ "Rhythm is Gonna Get You" was released in 1987 by who?**

Answer: Gloria Estefan and the Miami Sound Machine (This song peaked at #5 and was released from the album "Let It Loose")

**130/ What band released the song "Don't You Want Me" in 1981?**

Answer: Human League (Human League had the #6 song of 1982 in the U.S. and spent 5 consecutive weeks at #1 in the UK. It was released from their album "Dare")

**131/ What singer covered the Umberto Tozzi song "Gloria" in 1982?**

Answer: Laura Branigan ("Gloria" was originally released by the Italian co-writer Umberto Tozzi in 79. Van Morrison had a song by the same name in 1964)

**132/ "The Living Years" was released in 1988 by what group?**

Answer: Mike + the Mechanics (Mike + The Mechanics Hit #1 on both the Hot 100 and the Adult Contemporary charts in the U.S. It was the title song from their album)

**133/ What male singer released the song "All Those Years Ago" in 1981?**

Answer George Harrison (This was a tribute song to John Lennon by George Harrison teamed up with former band members Paul McCartney and Ring Starr on Drums.

**134/ "Cum On Feel The Noize" was originally released in 1973 by what band?**

Answer: Slade (Slade spent 4 weeks at #1 in the UK but only hit #98 on the U.S. Billboard charts in 1973. Quiet Riot covered the song in 1983 peaking at #5 in the U.S.)

**135/ Who released "(Just Like) Starting Over" in 1980?**

Answer: John Lennon (This was the #4 song of 1980 by John Lennon. It spent 1 week at #1 in the UK and was knocked off the top spot by "There's No One Quite Like Grandma" by the St. Winifred's school choir)

**136/ The "Sultans of Swing" was released in 1978 by what band?**

Answer: Dire Straits (Released from their first album titled "Dire Straits", the song peaked at #8 in the U.K. and #4 in the U.S. charts)

**137/ Who released the 1971 song "Draggin' The Line"?**

Answer: Tommy James (This was a solo release by Tommy James after the breakup from the Shondells in 1970)

**138/ Who released the song "Dancing on the Ceiling" in 1986?**

Answer: Lionel Richie (All 4 recorded the song but it was the Lionel Richie version that hit #2 on the charts. This song was the title track from his album becoming the #39 song of 1986)

**139/ "Let My Love Open The Door" was released in 1980 by who?**

Answer: Pete Townshend (Pete Townshend released the song from his album titled "Empty Glass" peaking at #9 in the U.S. and #46 in the U.K)

**140/ The song "Ghostbusters" was released in 1984 by who?**

Answer: Ray Parker Jr. (Released on the "Ghostbusters" soundtrack and became the #9 song of 1984)

**141/ Finish the lyrics to the 1989 song "The Look" by Roxette "Walking like a man, hitting like a hammer, She's a juvenile scam, ____ ____ ____ ____ "**

Answer: "Never was a quitter" (Roxette released the song from their album "Look Sharp!" and became the #17 bestselling song of 1989)

**142/ The #2 bestselling song of 1988 "Need You Tonight" was released in 1987 by who?**

Answer: INXS ("Need You Tonight" would become the only INXS song to reach #1 on the Billboard Hot 100 as of 2010. It was released from their album "Kick")

**143/ Name the group who had the #1 hit "Down Under" in 1983?**

Answer: Men At Work ("Down Under" became the #4 song of 1983 and it spent 3 consecutive weeks at #1 in the UK)

**144/ Who originally released the song "The Night The Lights Went Out In Georgia" in 1972?**

Answer: Vicki Lawrence (The song was released as a single with "Dime a Dance". It was later covered by Reba McEntire in 1991)

**145/ What band released the song "Come On Eileen" in 1983?**

Answer: Dexy's Midnight Runners (Dexys Midnight Runners had the #13 song of the year 1982 in the U.S. and spent 4 consecutive weeks at #1 in the UK. It was released from their album "Too-Rye-Ay")

**146/ Who released the #7 bestselling song of 1989 titled "Wind Beneath My Wings"?**

Answer: Bette Midler (Bette Midler released the song from "The Beaches" Soundtrack.)

**147/ In the 1989 song "My Prerogative" by Bobby Brown, In the second verse what was his response to the first line "They Say I'm Crazy"?**

Answer: "I really don't care" (The line goes "They say I'm crazy I really don't care" The song was released from his album "Don't Be Cruel" and became the #2 song of 1989)

**148/ Finish the missing lyrics from the 1987 George Michael song "Faith" "Oh but I need some time off from that emotion. Time to pick my____ ____ off the floor"**

Answer: Heart Up (This was the title track from the album which hit #1 in the U.S. and #2 in the U.K. becoming the #1 bestselling song of 1988)

**149/ Who released "Open Your Heart" in 1987?**

Answer: Madonna (This song hit #1 on the Billboard charts and became the #30 bestselling song of 1987. It was released from her "True Blue" album)

**150/ Who released the song "Jessie's Girl" in 1981?**

Answer: Rick Springfield (Released on his album "Working Class Dog" Hitting #1 on the U.S. charts for 2 weeks and became the #5 song of 1981)

**151/ Who released the song "Bohemian Rhapsody in 1975?**

Answer: Queen (The Queen song was originally released in 1975 but then again in 1992 after appearing in the film "Wayne's World")

**152/ In 1973 what group released the song "Tie A Yellow Ribbon 'Round The Ole Oak Tree"?**

Answer: Tony Orlando and Dawn (The song was released as a single with "I Can't Believe How Much I Love you" as the B-side)

**153/ In 1988, what metal band released the song "Every Rose Has Its Thorn"?**

Answer: Poison (Poison released the song from their album "Open Up and Say Ahh!" hitting #1 on Christmas Eve. 1988 and holding for 3 weeks)

**154/ What song did Dave Edmunds cover on the album "Rockpile" in 1970?**

Answer: - "I Hear You Knocking" (Edmunds cover of "I Hear You Knocking" spent 6 weeks at #1 in the UK and peaked at #4 in the U.S. The song was originally released by Smiley Lewis in 1955)

**155/ What female singer released "Morning Train (Nine to Five)" in 1981?**

Answer: Sheena Easton (Originally titled "9 to 5", it was renamed "Morning Train" to avoid confusion in the U.S. with the Dolly Parton song which was released at the same time. Sheen Easton released her song from her "Take My Time" album)

**156/ What group released the song "Alive And Kicking" in 1986?**

Answer: Simple Minds (Released from their album "Once Upon a Time" The song peaked at #3 on the Billboard charts and #5 in the U.K.)

**157/ Who hit #21 on the Billboard charts for 1974 with their version of "Billy Don't Be A Hero"?**

Answer: Bo Donaldson and The Heywoods (The song was released by Paper Lace hitting #1 in the U.K. but before they could release the hit in the United States, Bo Donaldson recorded his version taking it to #1)

**158/ Who released the song "Arthur's Theme" in 1982?**

Answer: Christopher Cross (Christopher Cross co-wrote and released the song on "Arthur - The Album")

**159/ Name the song with the lyrics - "Life is a mystery, everyone can stand alone" (1989)**

Answer: "Like A Prayer" (Madonna spent 3 weeks at #1 with this song in the UK. It became the 25th bestselling song of 1989 in the U.S.)

**160/ Name the artist or group who had the #2 bestselling song of 1987 titled "Alone"?**

Answer: Heart ("Alone" topped the charts in the U.S. and Canada while it peaked at #3 in the UK. It was released as a single with the live version of "Barracuda" as the B-side)

**161/ What group released the song "Get Down Tonight" in 1975?**

Answer: KC and the Sunshine Band (Released from their self-titled album, with "You Don't Know" as the B-side hitting #1 in the U.S.)

**162/ Name the artist/group who covered the song "Baby, I Love your Way" in 1989?**

Answer: Will to Power (The song was released by Frampton in 1975 then covered by Will to Power in 1989 and then again by Big Mountain in 1994)

**163/ Who had the #1 hit song in 1984 titled "I Just Called To Say I Love You"?**

Answer: Stevie Wonder (Stevie Wonder spent 6 weeks at #1 in the U.K. while it became the #25 bestselling song of the year in the U.S.)

**164 "Party All The Time" was released in 1985 by who?**

Answer: Eddie Murphy (Eddie Murphy released the song from his album "How Could It Be". It was written and produced by Rick James)

**165/ Who released the #1 bestselling song of 1984 titled "Careless Whisper"?**

Answer: Wham (This was the first solo release by George Michael but was credited to Wham and released from their album "Make It Big")

**166/ Name the group that released "Crazy Little Thing Called Love" in 1979?**

Answer: Queen (This was released from their album "The Game" spending 4 weeks at #1 in the U.S. and 7 weeks at #1 in Australia. It was also a #1 hit for country singer Dwight Yoakam on the Canadian RPM country Tracks)

**167/ Who released the song "R.O.C.K. In The U.S.A." in 1985?**

Answer: John Mellencamp (The song peaked at #2 and was released from his album "Scarecrow")

**168/ Who released the song "You Light Up My Life" in 1978?**

Answer: Debby Boone (This was the title track of the album and set a record for spending 10 weeks at #1 on the Billboard Hot 100 charts)

**169/ What group released the 1973 song "Takin' Care Of Business"?**

Answer: Bachman-Turner Overdrive (Bachman-Turner Overdrive released the song from their album "Bachman-Turner Overdrive II")

**170/ Name The Song with the lyrics - "Jeremiah was a bullfrog, was a good friend of mine. I never understood a single word he said, but I helped him a-drink his wine" (1970)**

Answer: "Joy To The World" ("Joy To The World held #1 for 6 weeks and became the Billboard Hot 100 Number one song of the year 1971 for Three Dog Night. It was released as a single with "I Can Hear You Calling" as the B-side)

**171/ In 1986, who released the song "Rock Me Amadeus"?**

Answer: Falco (Falco released the song from his "Falco 3" album. It spent 1 week at the top of the charts in the U.K. and became the #28 bestselling song in the U.S)

**172/ Name the singer or group that released the song titled "The Long Run" in 1979?**

Answer: The Eagles ("The Long Run" was the title track from the Eagles album peaking at #8 on the U.S. charts)

**173/ Who released the song titled "Neutron Dance" in 1984?**

Answer: Pointer Sisters (The Pointer Sisters released this song from their debut album "Break Out")

**174/ The song "Call Me" was released in 1980 by what band?**

Answer: Blondie (This was used as the theme song from the film "American Gigolo". It hit #1 in the U.S. becoming the #1 song of 1980. It also hit #1 Canada and U.K. and #2 in Australia)

**175/ Name the singer who took "Ricky Don't Lose That Number" to #51 in 1974?**

Answer: Steely Dan (Released as a single with "Any Major Dude Will Tell You" as the B-side and from his album "Pretzel Logic")

**176/ Who released the 1973 song "Sunshine On My Shoulders"?**

Answer: John Denver (The song was Co-written by John Denver and released from his album "Poems, Prayers & Promises" hitting #1 in the U.S.)

**177/ "Things Can Only Get Better" was released in 1985 by who?**

Answer: Howard Jones (Howard Jones released the song from his "Dream Into Action" album)

**178/ "Hit Me With Your Best Shot" was released in 1980 By what female singer?**

Answer: Pat Benatar (This song was released from her "Crimes Of Passion Album")

**179/ The song "Church Of The Poison Mind" was released in 1983 by what group?**

Answer: Culture Club ("Church of the Poison Mind" was released from their "Colour by Numbers" album becoming the #82 song of 1984)

**180/ The song "Celebration" was released in 1980 by who?**

Answer: Kool and the Gang ("Celebration" spent 6 weeks at #1 on the Billboard Hot 100 charts and was the #6 song of 1981. It was released from their album "Celebrate!")

**181/ Name the song with the lyrics - "When you're weary, feeling small. When tears are in your eyes, I will dry them all" (1970)**

Answer: "Bridge Over Troubled Water" (This was the title song from the Simon and Garfunkel album and held the #1 position for 6 consecutive weeks)

**182/ According to the 1972 song "My Ding-A-Ling", who bought him a cute little toy?**

Answer: Grandma (The song by Chuck Berry spent 4 weeks at #1 in the UK and became his only #1 hit in the US holding the top spot for 1 week)

**183/ In the 1985 Dire Straits song "Money for Nothing" what is it they say was free in the line "Money for Nothing and the _____ for free"?**

Answer: Chicks (Dire Straits made this the #8 song of 1985 and was released from their album titled "Brothers In Arms)

**184/ Name the artist who released the #1 song "Papa Don't Preach" in 1986?**

Answer: Madonna (The song spent 3 weeks at #1 in the U.K and was the #29 bestselling song of 1986 in the U.S.)

**185/ In 1979, who released the song "We Don't Talk Anymore"?**

Answer: Cliff Richard (Cliff Richard spent 4 weeks at #1 in the UK and peaked at #7 in the U.S. It was released from his album "Rock 'n' Roll juvenile")

**186/ Footloose was released in 1984 by what singer?**

Answer: Kenny Loggins (Kenny Loggins made this the #4 bestselling song of 1984 and was released from the soundtrack "Footloose")

**187/ Name the song with the lyrics - "I don't want to talk, about things we've gone through. Though it's hurting me now it's history" (1980)**

Answer: "The Winner Takes It All" (Abba spent 2 weeks at #1 in the UK and was the #23 song of 1980 in the U.S.)

**188/ Who had the #1 song in 1978 titled "Three Times A Lady"?**

Answer: The Commodores (The Commodores spent 5 consecutive weeks at #1 in the UK was the #10 song of the year in the U.S. Lionel Richie was the Lead singer for the Commodores)

**189/ What group released the song "Rock And Roll All Nite" in 1975?**

Answer: Kiss (From their album "Dressed To Kill" the song peaked at #12 in the U.S. and #18 in Australia but still was ranked the #16 greatest hard rock song of all time by VH1 in 2008 )

**190/ "Say You Say Me" was released in 1986 by who?**

Answer: Lionel Richie (The song was recorded for the film "White Nights" and released from the Lionel Richie album "Dancing on the Ceiling" becoming the #2 Bestselling song of 1986)

**191/ Name the group who released the 1976 song "You Sexy Thing"?**

Answer: Hot Chocolate (The song was released from their self-titled album and hit #2 in the U.K. and #3 in the U.S. It gained recognition after being featured in the 1997 film "The Full Monty")

**192/ Name the song with the lyrics - "Funny how it seems, always in time, but never in line for dreams". (1983)?**

Answer: True ("True spent 4 consecutive weeks at #1 in the UK and Barely made it into the top 100 bestselling songs of 1983 reaching #92 in the U.S.)

**193/ Who released the song "Spiders And Snakes" in 1973?**

Answer: Jim Stafford (This was Stafford's most successful recording hitting #1 in Canada and #3 in the U.S.)

**194/ Who covered the song "Greatest Love Of All" making it the #11 bestselling song of 1986?**

Answer: Whitney Houston (The song was released by George Benson in 1977 and covered by Whitney Houston in 1986. It was released from her self-titled album)

**195/ What Band released "Look Away in 1988?**

Answer: Chicago (Chicago released this song on their album "Chicago 19" where it became the bestselling song of 1989)

**196/ Name the song with the lyrics - "Promise me son, not to do the things I've done. Walk away from trouble if you can" (1980)**

- " Answer: "Coward of the County" (The Kenny Rogers song "The Coward of the County" was the #34 song of 1980 in the U.S. It spent 2 weeks at #1 in the UK)

**197/ What group released the song "I'll Take You There" in 1972?**

Answer: The Staple Singers (Soul/Gospel group The Staple Singers released "I'll Take You There" from their album "Be Altitude: Respect Yourself")

**198/ Name the Actor who had the hit song in 1977 titled "Don't Give Up On Us"?**

Answer: David Soul (David Soul from Starsky and Hutch spent 4 weeks at #1 in the UK and was the #29 bestselling song of the year in the U.S.)

**199/ Who covered the 1968 song "Red Red Wine" hitting the #1 position in 1983?**

Answer: UB40 ("UB40 Spent 3 weeks at #1 in the UK and was the #39 bestselling song of 1983 in the U.S. It was released from their album "Labour of Love" Originally written and released by Neil Diamond)

**200/ The song "Sara Smile" was the #11 song for 1976 and was sung by who?**

Answer: Hall & Oates (Released from their first album titled "Daryl Hall & John Oates")

**201/ What Group released the song "25 Or 6 To 4" in 1970?**

Answer: Chicago (With Peter Cetera on lead vocals, this song peaked at #4 on the Billboard Hot 100 and #7 in the U.K. It was released as a single with "Where Do We Go From Here" as the B-side)

**202/ Name the #1 hit song from 1970 with the lyrics "When no-one else can understand me. When everything I do is wrong"?**

Answer: The Wonder Of You (The song was released by Ray Peterson in 1959 and covered by Elvis Presley in 1970 when it spent 6 weeks at #1 in the UK but peaked at #7 in the U.S.)

**203/ Who released the 1981 song "Chariots Of Fire"?**

Answer: Vangelis (Vangelis recorded the song for the "Chariots Of Fire" Soundtrack)

**204/ Who released the song "If You Don't Know Me By Now" in 1972?**

Answer: Harold Melvin & the Blue Notes (Harold Melvin & the Blue Notes topped the R&B charts and came in at #3 on the Pop charts in 1972. Simply Red covered the song in 1989)

**205/ Who released the song titled "Out Of Touch" in 1984?**

Answer: Hall and Oates (Daryl Hall and John Oates or Hall & Oates released the song from their album "Big Bam Boom". It was the #6 song for the year)

**206/ In 1970, who released the song called "In The Summertime"?**

Answer: Mungo Jerry (Mungo Jerry spent 7 consecutive weeks at #1 in the UK and 2 weeks at #1 in Canada but peaked at #3 on the Billboard Hot 100)

**207/ What female singer released the song "You're So Vain" in 1972?**

Answer: Carly Simon (Carly Simon wrote and released "You're So Vain" spending 3 weeks at #1 in the U.S. and was from her album titled "No Secrets")

**208/ Name the song with the lyrics - "First I was afraid I was petrified. Kept thinking I could never live without you by my side" (1978)**

Answer: "I Will Survive" (Gloria Gaynor spent 4 weeks at #1 in the UK and became the #6 bestselling song of 1979 in the U.S.)

**209/ Name the Song with the lyrics - "I never seen you looking so lovely as you did tonight? (1986)**

Answer: "Lady In Red" ("Lady In Red" spent 3 consecutive weeks at #1 in the UK and was the #21 song of 1987 in the United States.)

Made in the USA
Middletown, DE
15 December 2021